# TURNING

## MY PAIN INTO PURPOSE

### A Book Of
### Inspirational Poems

By: Janae C.

# Dedication

I want to dedicate this book to God. Thank you for helping me and saving my life. Also, this book is for people out there who feel alone; know that God will bring you through anything, and prayer changes everything. I wrote these poems through my healing journey. Hopefully, these poems can help you through whatever you have experienced or are currently facing.

# Table of Contents

Dedication..................................................................................................i

Chapter 1: Love..........................................................................................1

Chapter 2: Soul Ties...................................................................................2

Chapter 3: Why Her....................................................................................3

Chapter 4: Husband....................................................................................4

Chapter 5: Beautiful Woman......................................................................5

Chapter 6: Dear Dad...................................................................................6

Chapter 7: Dear God...................................................................................7

Chapter 8: Self Love....................................................................................8

Chapter 9: Toxic........................................................................................10

Chapter 10: A Bleeding Heart..................................................................12

Chapter 11: 5 am Sessions........................................................................13

Chapter 12: Forbidden Fruit....................................................................14

Chapter 13: Wounds Are Wisdom...........................................................15

Chapter 14: Verbal Abuse.........................................................................17

Chapter 15: Speak.....................................................................................18

Chapter 16: Love Languages.....................................................................19

Chapter 17: Days Of The Week................................................................20

Chapter 18: Crush.....................................................................................21

Chapter 19: Random Conversations.........................................................22

Chapter 20: Hidden Jewels.......................................................................23

Chapter 21: Las Vegas...............................................................................24

Chapter 22: Why Would He Fail You?.....................................................25

Chapter 23: Unspoken Words...................................................................26

# Chapter 1: Love

Love so many things.
I have to tell you, happiness, pain, and tears are all I feel.
Do u truly know what true love is
because lust and love both feel so real?

Love, I always fell for the wrong guy,
being so shy, not seeing their soul straight through their eyes.
Love, I'm ashamed because this thing called love isn't just a game,
because playing with someone's heartstrings sometimes makes you go mentally insane.

Love is supposed to be kind,
gentle, and simple,
and most importantly, honoring your temple.

Love, so the next time you think you have found true love
ask yourself if it is real
because true love truly makes you heal.

# Chapter 2: Soul Ties

**Soul ties.**
It's an energy exchange
because when you lay down with someone,
it will never be the same.

Soul ties are thinking you know someone.
But you don't have a clue
because creating soul ties
will make you create illusions in your head
that will never come true.

Soul ties will make you feel like you're on cloud 9,
but when reality hits,
it will feel like a train running off the tracks
and not knowing who it will attack,
and then all you hear is smack;
that's a fact.

Soul ties are so dangerous,
and that's a fact.
So the next time you lay with someone
don't get attached.

# Chapter 3: Why Her

**Why her?**
I never thought I would ask myself that
because I thought our bond was as deep as the ocean goes.

**Why her?**
I gave you my time, patience,
and, most importantly, my heart,
so now I'm torn apart.

**Why her?**
You could have told me
that you never thought of me like that.

**Why her?**
Because it's a fact
that I couldn't do the things that made your heart sing,
so now my heart feels so broken like piano strings.

**Why her?**
I had to think I was enough,
but the truth is
your touch was so full of lust
that my body should have never touched.

**Why her?**
Then I had to realize — why not,
because he just wasn't for me,
so that's how I got to grieve properly.

# Chapter 4: Husband

**Looking for you**
in all the wrong places,
looking for you
in all the wrong faces.

I know when I find you,
I will lose control
because as soon I look into your eyes,
you will snatch my soul.

**Looking for you,**
the way you will touch me,
it will feel like an out-of-body experience,
like I'm in two different dimensions.

**Looking for you,**
my heart will heal,
and I will begin to feel
because your love will reveal
what it truly means to heal,
and that's for real.

**Looking for you,**
one day we shall meet.
There's a scripture that says,
"Seek, and you will find,"
so our love will be divine.

**Looking for you,**
the stars will align,
and when I find you,
it will be destined from the Divine.

# Chapter 5: Beautiful Woman

**Beautiful woman,**
through all the struggles that you have been through,
you still smile.

**Beautiful woman,**
it's okay that the pain you felt
turned into a testimony.

**Beautiful woman,**
that smile lights up like 1000 stars
in a universe that only God can bring.

**Beautiful woman,**
your aura is like a beautiful garden
with a sudden breeze rolling past your knees.

**Beautiful**
always feel whole with self-control
because what matter's the most
is what is in your soul.

**Beautiful woman,**
happiness comes from the inside,
and that's something not everyone knows.

**Beautiful woman,**
so stay confident
and keep your head held high
because you are a beautiful woman.

# Chapter 6: Dear Dad

**Dear Dad,**
the day you left this world,
it was tears that I couldn't bear.

**Dear Dad,**
even though we didn't always see eye to eye,
you raised me,
and that's alright.

**Dear Dad,**
all I feel is pain,
and my tears became full like a lake,
so now my heart aches.
I can't take it,
and so I will instantly break.

**Dear Dad,**
I will never forget those talks that we used to have,
laughing all day on the phone
until the sunset.

**Dear Dad,**
I know the pain will never go away,
but God will help me get through every day.

I will always love you, Dad.
Your daughter,
**Janae.**

# Chapter 7: Dear God

**Dear God,**
I just love you so much;
without you, my heart will stop.

**Dear God,**
thank you for loving me
even when I couldn't love myself.

**Dear God,**
you know all that my heart desires
and my thoughts.
You gave me blessings
that turned into lessons
that I thought I wanted.

**Dear God,**
it's an honor to be in your presence
because of who you are.
Without you, I would be rotting away like tooth decay,
and my soul would be far away.

**Dear God,**
thank you for being my father,
protector,
friend,
and most importantly, just you.
I love you, God.

# Chapter 8: Self Love

When you look at yourself,
what do you see?
We always say we love ourselves,
but do we truly know what that means?

Every time I look in the mirror,
I see a flaw.
I thought I knew what self-love was,
but actually, I didn't really know at all.

Seeing flaws every day,
I look in the mirror
and never knew life could be so hard.
I am tired of getting mistreated
and broken into pieces,
trying to find peace.

I don't know where to start,
but all I know is I want me back.
I am stuck in between,
so now it's me vs me.

## Reflection
my life is truly a blessing.
Self-love suddenly becomes a lesson.
I am stressing and learning as I go,
but life is truly a lesson.

## God, don't leave me;
I am begging and hitting the floor.
I fantasize about the person I used to be before
without realizing I never learned the new me.

Then I got to thinking —
I had been through so much;
the new me deserves a hug
as much as the old me
because I made it.

God, I realized you wanted me grow.
I then became teary-eyed
and dropped down to my knees,
begging God.

I had realized
that self-love comes from God,
then His grace comes to me;
and that —
that's how I obtained peace.

# Chapter 9: Toxic

**Toxic.**
I don't hate you,
but the truth is it's hard.
You never knew how much you hurt me.
I'm crying,
can't eat,
and don't know how to sleep
dreaming about you and me.

Trying to pray to keep the faith
the pastor says every Sunday,
but every time I see your face,
my heart goes into dismay.

Never knew you could hurt me
as bad as you did,
but you did.
Whew, was that a thought?
Naw, that was my reality.

My heart feels like it's about to stop,
and I have to face the fact
that letting you go
wasn't just a train of thought.

Still can't believe
I had to learn the hard way
what toxicity means.

So, now I look around
at family and friends;
my heart is conflicted,
not knowing what to do:
should I stay in this situation
or let these people break me?

I have to change;
I must change.
So, I prayed for better days.

I'm losing my mind;
it's like I'm in the matrix
and can't find my way out.

Then God came to my heart and said,
**"Let them go.**
**I'm going to take the pain away."**

I cried on my knees,
begging God, please.
Then I felt a chill.
I began to let go.
I finally started to feel free.
There were no more shackles on me.

# Chapter 10: A Bleeding Heart

So many things I wish I could tell you.
I really miss you.
I hope you miss me too.

I'm thinking about the day I met you.
Man, that smile is so beautiful,
just like your soul.
Around you, I don't have no self-control.

They say when you lose something,
you have to let it go,
but if it comes back,
it means so much more.

The crazy thing about a heart is
when it stops, it's bleed's,
shattered like a piece of glass.
I know this, too, shall pass.

I never meant to fall for you.
I'm like a dismantled doll
trying to get put back together,
but it won't fit.
I know my feelings were legit.

I miss our conversations.
Most of all,
you put vitality back in my body;
I would have risked it all.

The stars weren't aligned,
and that's okay.
I just hope
that we will be back friends someday.

But until then,
it's goodbye.
I can't believe I shed tears
because I thought you were that guy.

# Chapter 11: 5 am Sessions

**It's 5 am,**
and I woke up out of my sleep.
I have so much on my mind,
so it's hard for me to be at peace.

**5 am,**
thinking about all the pain that I have been through.
Man, it's hard for me to cope.
I just need to pray to God,
so my knees hit the floor.
I never felt like this before.

**5 am,**
everybody sleeps but me.
So, I lay there,
even though I'm in a world full of people,
I feel so alone, man.
I can't do this on my own.

**5 am,**
I'm breaking,
then I got to shaking because of my anxiety;
I pray I heal properly.

**5 am,**
wanting to accomplish my dreams,
but when I take a step forward,
I get knocked back down
like a game named Jenga.
I really need to fix my crown.

**5 am,**
I wish I could scream for joy,
then I prayed for peace.
I felt a breeze;
that's how I knew God was watching over me.

# Chapter 12: Forbidden Fruit

**Him,**
the way those brown eyes are just so sexy,
I wish he could be mine.

**Him,**
we started off as close friends.
Man, you see through me like a looking glass.
You carry yourself with so much class;
you kept it real, and that's all I ever asked.

**Him,**
the only thing you require is for me to be me.
That's the realist thing that someone ever said to me.

**Him,**
I always see the best in you
even when you don't see it in yourself;
don't change you for nobody else.

**Him,**
our conversations be dope;
I hope our friendship constantly grows.

**Him,**
you teach me how to be straightforward.
Man, I just love your aura.
It's like when the sun comes up in the morning;
such a beautiful sight.

**Him,**
we understand each other.
It's so scary,
but the truth is it's like a twisted robe
that's stuck together like glue.

**Him,**
maybe if only you knew how deeply I care for you.

# Chapter 13: Wounds Are Wisdom

**Wounds are wisdom;**
life is a mess,
but it's part of the process,
so why stress when you are blessed?

**Wounds are wisdom.**
Even though you have that scar,
it will heal in time,
and you will be fine
because one thing about the divine
is that He is always on time.

**Wounds are wisdom.**
Don't second guess the journey
because you are worthy;
release control,
and you will grow
because that's the ultimate goal.

**Wounds are wisdom.**
They say time can heal all wounds,
which is true,
but you have to go through
those trials and tribulations
that don't define you.

**Wounds are wisdom.**
Why stress when life is tested
to bring out the best,
and those times will be priceless.

**Wounds are wisdom.**
God always will fulfill His promises.
It's just His time,
so be patient,
because one thing about the divine
is that He will give you strength
to get through a difficult time.

**Wounds are wisdom.**
You won't fail;
you will prevail
as long as you keep moving.
You will excel,
and that is what will bring wisdom.

# Chapter 14: Verbal Abuse

**Verbal abuse is so damaging.**
If only you knew how you made me feel.

**Verbal abuse,**
you think when you call me bitches and hoes,
they are relationship goals,
but it's really toxic.
I wonder, do you really know?

**Verbal abuse,**
just because I don't agree,
doesn't make me stupid,
but to be honest,
I am really foolish going in this cycle.
I really need to get into my Bible.

**Verbal abuse:**
I wonder if I changed myself,
would it be enough for you?
But the truth is,
your flesh overpowers your spirit,
so how can I expect you to honor your temple?

**Verbal abuse,**
you go off emotions.
It's like an ocean with never-ending water.

**Verbal abuse,**
it's never okay.
Don't let someone damage you
and take your vitality away.

# Chapter 15: Speak

**Speak from the heart**
even when life feels like it's getting torn apart.
**Speak from your soul**
because once you open your mouth,
the gentle tone connected to your spirit
won't stir you the wrong way.

**Speak strong**
because what we might like is actually wrong.
**Speak,**
let your soul breathe,
and then you will find peace.

**Speak,**
open up your mouth,
and speak your truth
because the only one you are holding captive is you.

**Speak,**
stop being miserable.
It's time to release the burden of always being perfect,
and it will be worth it.

**Speak,**
free yourself,
and that is how you will obtain spiritual wealth.

# Chapter 16: Love Languages

Love languages:
**physical touch** – when you touch my skin and touch my soul,
that's what I call spiritual goals.

Love languages:
**affirmations** are so beautiful
because you are speaking to the soul,
but truth be told,
what you feed your soul will constantly grow.
That's how you will know God is always in control.

Love languages:
**receiving gifts** – it's such a beautiful thing
because there's nothing like giving to someone without any strings,
you know what I mean?

Love languages:
**quality time** is like a garden
because once you plant your seeds,
you can watch them grow.
Spending quality time is how you truly get to know someone
and strengthen your bond.
Ultimately, your relationship will grow.

Love languages:
**acts of service** are so kind, gentle, and most of all selfless
because to give is one of the most precious things,
and best believe you will get to the heartstrings.

**Love languages** are so beautiful
when you truly feel that feeling.
So, when you finally feel that love,
that's how you know you obtained true commitment.

# Chapter 17: Days of the Week

**Monday,**
the start of a new week and the start of a new you.

**Tuesday,**
waking up and talking to God
because His promises and faithfulness are always true.

**Wednesday,**
knowing God is in control,
even when you can't see His vision.
You are exactly where you need to be on this journey.

**Thursday,**
manifesting your dreams even when it seems far,
but knowing God is all things, so He can do it all.

**Friday,**
always remember that it's divine timing,
so dream big and believe it's going to happen.
Stop stressing, it's messing with your mental,
and it will also damage your temple.

Let's not forget, it's finally **Saturday,**
so get ready for the weekend.
Let's be right within because being beautiful on the outside and not on the inside matters,
because the outside is just a vessel, but our spirit lives on forever.

**Sunday** is our Sabbath day to become centered,
but also to self-reflect.
At the end of the week, we speak and praise God in advance.
Let's spend the days of the week happy, grateful,
blessing others, healing within,
spreading knowledge to help others,
being grateful for the small things,
smiling, and most importantly, praising God for just being Him.
That's our Father, He is all things!

# Chapter 18: Crush

I'm crushing on you so much
that when you smile, my heart melts away.
It feels like I'm winning the Powerball
on any given Saturday.

Crush, our conversations be so deep,
you got me swept off my feet.
I feel like I'm floating on water
and I can't drown because the love I have for you is so deep.

Crush, I thought it was lust,
but that gentle hug has my body shaking.
It feels like my bones are breaking,
man, I can't take it, so I'll embrace it.

Crush, the way you understand me is so incredible,
it's like I'm looking in the mirror at my self-reflection.
Meeting you was a blessing,
and the other guys I ran into were a lesson.

Crush, thanks for the laughter,
the talks, and most importantly, your friendship,
my forever crush.

# Chapter 19: Random Conversations

Hit different from the way you look at me,
I can't believe I just met you so randomly.
Hit different, this conversation feels like I've known you for years.
Man, I wish I could have held back all those dang tears.

Hit different, you so fine,
you got me biting on my bottom lip,
got my soul feeling like a golden ticket.
Hit different, everything you say is just so accurate,
that's what makes you so attractive.

Hit different, your aura is king vibes,
I gotta watch myself so I don't create soul ties
and I'm not speaking any lies.
Hit different, in a room full of people it's only us;
man, our vibes got the mightiest touch.

You hit different, and that's a fact.
I never got to ask your name
because the truth about this dating game
is that when we officially exchange numbers,
it won't never be the same.

# Chapter 20: Hidden Jewels

Hidden jewels are so precious.
God gives us all gifts to help us live our best life, don't you think?
We are here on this Earth for a purpose,
so find your hidden jewel and use it to blossom,
to see your gift come to life.

We may not realize or even seek them,
but I do know whatever it is, God made it just for me.
So why would I blend in?
I call something like that "the blend in game."
That's what I'm calling it.

I should have solved it, but it hasn't been done.
I'm praying and fasting so God can show me.
I'm anxious and nervous because I want to live up to my potential.

But I have to remember hidden gems are always hidden in long-lost treasure,
so I will medicate, fast, and pray
because I know one day God is going to open the vault.

# Chapter 21: Las Vegas

One day in Las Vegas,
you would think I would be excited, but I wasn't.
One day in Las Vegas,
I saw how beautiful it was,
but for me, it was a dark day.

One day in Las Vegas,
my heart was filled with pain.
My dad died; my world was turned upside down,
and all I could do was put my head down.

One day in Las Vegas,
I'm driving to see my dad,
he's really dead,
I can't get you out of my head,
and all I keep seeing is your corpse lying in that casket bed.

One day in Las Vegas,
it felt like a nightmare,
but it was my reality.
I wish I could rewind time like a cassette tape;
it put me in a bad state.

One day in Las Vegas,
I'm seeing flashing lights on the strip,
everyone was happy but me.
I can't believe I lost the man who raised me.

One day in Las Vegas,
I felt crushed, didn't even want to be touched.
I had so much anxiety,
I pray, I hope I grieve properly.

One day in Las Vegas,
seeing you lying there cold as ice,
you wanted to obtain peace there,
but at what price?

One day in Las Vegas,
I prayed for God to give me strength,
because my vitality felt gone.
God, I felt so alone.

# Chapter 22: Why Would He Fail You?

Why would He fail you?
Has He ever?
God, when I think about you,
I feel such peace.
I never knew somebody could love me the way that you do,
so why would He fail you?

God, you brought me so far in life,
I am not the same person I was before.
I'm better,
so why would He fail you?

God, you keep my mind at ease
when life gets too much for me,
you help me find peace,
so why would He fail you?

God, you've been with me
when I didn't have a place to stay,
I was homeless, no money, no income,
and You came through and made a way,
so why would He fail you?

Never question the power of the Lord.
If He did it before,
He will do it again.
The power of prayer is deep within!

# Chapter 23: Unspoken Words

Friends became foes.
God took them away when I released control.
Nurturing my soul, that's what I call friendship goals.

I learned life can be a bit lonely on your journey.
But the truth is, God is here, and He will reveal who you should let go of so you can truly heal.

I learned a hard nose makes a soft ass; the way the elders say it be with so much class.
Having wisdom is so beautiful yet so hard.
Because the more you know, your flesh will test you
It's like waiting at the bus stop, but it never comes.
But with faith, the bus will always run.

I'm a wife, nothing less. I'm learning my value, and that was a test, but that's what made it priceless.

I'm learning to pour into myself more and more every day since I started to pray.
The more I pour into my cup, it tilts over, and that's okay.
That is because I'm healing not the physical, but the spiritual
I hope y'all caught this shift going on in my mental.

www.ingramcontent.com/pod-product-compliance
Lightning Source LLC
Chambersburg PA
CBHW041131120626
46547CB00019B/2944